A Jump-Rope Song

by Iris Littleman
illustrated by Albert Molnar

Y0-DKP-023

Harcourt

Orlando   Boston   Dallas   Chicago   San Diego

Jumping rope is fun to do.
We will swing the rope for you.

We swing fast. We do not stop.
In you jump. Out you hop.

Now you can jump and hop again.

Jump and hop from 1 to 10!

We will sing this jump-rope song.

We will jump the whole day long!

One o'clock, two o'clock.
The king sat on a stone.

Three o'clock, four o'clock.
He gave his dog a bone.

Five o'clock, six o'clock.
The king got up. He rose.

Now it's time to jump and hop.
Put your hand on your nose!

Jumping rope is fun to do.
We hope that it was fun for you!